51 Things Every Actor Should Know

Bobby Lacer

Writer/Producer/Director/Actor
Little Chicago Pictures, CEO

51 Things Every Actor Should Know
By **Bobby Lacer**

Burning Bulb Publishing
P.O. Box 4721
Bridgeport, WV 26330-4721
United States of America
www.BurningBulbPublishing.com

Copyright © 2024 Bobby Lacer.
All rights reserved.

First Edition.

Paperback Edition ISBN: 978-1-964172-07-1

TABLE OF CONTENTS

FOREWORD 1

INTRODUCTION 3

AUDITIONS 5

COACHING & TRAINING 7

FACE THE ADVERSITY 9

GETTING WORK 11

HEADSHOTS 13

RÉSUMÉ 17

SELF TAPING 19

TECHNOLOGY 21

WRAP-UP 23

101 TERMS EVERY ACTOR SHOULD KNOW 25

FOREWORD

51 Things Every Actor Should Know was compiled by multi-award-winning writer, producer, director, and actor – Bobby Lacer. He intends to educate anyone interested in learning more about the art of acting.

I first met Bobby in 2018 when I was cast to play his real-life son's onscreen dad in a Ford commercial. I only had one word to say, but had to deliver it 20 different ways. From my first moments on set, Bobby was welcoming, encouraging, and more importantly... supportive. Throughout the years we have been blessed to work on many award-winning feature films and have grown our friendship both professionally and personally to the extent that I truly consider him family.

Whether he is teaching high school or college students, coaching young athletes, giving a speech at a seminar, or leading an acting class, it is obvious he truly loves being an educator. His knowledge of the acting industry is vast and only surpassed by his hope and desire to help others succeed in their career goals. Anyone who has ever worked with him knows that he strives for nothing less than perfection and his creative energy is truly contagious. This book is just one of his many passion projects and should serve as a guide to both aspiring and seasoned actors. I have been acting and commercial modeling for more than 20 years and every time I talk to Bobby, I still learn something new. He is always educating himself and trying to help others in all aspects of life because he cares about people.

I find the topic of 'Facing the Adversity' to be the section I refer back to most often. This business is very competitive and cutthroat, so being reminded to not get in your own way is always a wake-up call of sorts. An actor at any career level must be able to handle rejection and it's how they deal with being told 'no' that can certainly make or break an actor. I am guilty of having a wandering mind; Why didn't they pick me? What did I do wrong? Maybe I am just not good enough. Many acting coaches refer to these as BATS (bad actor thoughts) and it is common to blame others, get down on yourself, or second guess your performance choices, so facing adversity reminds me that I also need to have GATS (good actor thoughts) to stay in a more positive, reassuring mindset. Bobby has often told me, "There will always be someone better suited for a role than you, including future you." This alone has encouraged me to continue holding my head high and never stop learning and training.

Every actor's journey is different, but the information needed to be successful remains the same, regardless of how someone defines success. I challenge you to physically write out what a successful acting career means to you. The industry is changing faster these days than a screenwriter's thoughts can put pen to paper or fingers to a keyboard. This book is an excellent resource for every actor. I can attest that the information within these pages is essential, whether you are looking to jump-start your career or refresh your knowledge to bring you out of a booking slump; trust me, I know personally.

I lead you into this book with something I tell myself every day – Auditions are performances. Never skip an opportunity to perform.

James Dickey

James Dickey

James is a multi-award-winning actor who has appeared in numerous film and television shows, including *Fighting the Fire, Chicago Fire, C.I. Ape, Anything BUT Christmas, Freaky Profiling,* and *A Fireman for Christmas.*

INTRODUCTION

Every actor enters the business hoping to be an overnight success. Unfortunately, this is very rarely the case. Most actors spend years auditioning and taking minor roles for small pay to finally get their opportunity to play a big role in a major sitcom or motion picture.

While this is true, actors can increase their chances of being discovered sooner rather than later. Knowing the industry and how to set yourself up for the highest likelihood of success is the biggest part of the battle. Oftentimes, things that seem small or trivial are in reality very important stepping stones to your eventual success.

So, how do you properly prepare yourself to succeed? How do you put your best foot forward to be recognized by industry executives? And most importantly, how do you avoid the pitfalls that so many other actors fall into, only to find themselves deep in an abyss of endless failure that ultimately leads to their complete exit from the acting business? The answer comes down to one simple word – KNOWLEDGE.

Make no mistake about it, acting is a hard business. It's cut-throat and many (if not most) people are out for themselves. But there are good people in the industry. People who want to help you and see you succeed. Your success can often lead to their success. So setting yourself up to be recognized for your talent and commitment to your craft is exponentially important.

Talent can only take you so far. Your commitment to bettering yourself and growing as an actor will lead you further than you could ever imagine. But it takes time, dedication, confidence, resilience, effort, and know-how to survive and conquer.

Knowledge is power. Reside yourself to gather and gain as much knowledge about your craft as possible. Watch films, read industry books, listen to interviews with actors and directors, ask questions of other actors, work with acting coaches, do anything you can to consistently make yourself better.

51 Things Every Actor Should Know is designed to give you the knowledge and tools needed to enter this business fully armed and ready for battle. Take what you learn here and implement it into your everyday routine. This book provides the tools to succeed... the rest is up to you.

Bobby Lacer

AUDITIONS

1. **Casting directors ALWAYS want actors to succeed.**
   Study the character. Develop your take on the character. Show your true personality when you enter the audition. Allow them to like you, which gives you a strong chance at being memorable.

2. **Never be late for an audition.**
   Whether online or in person, never be late for an audition – NEVER. When meeting in person, you should ideally arrive at least 15-20 minutes before your scheduled audition time. Other actors may not show up and the casting team may be ahead of schedule. This will give you a chance to hit the audition room early and demonstrate you are not only prompt but likely to never be late for a call time on set.

3. **Memorize your lines.**
   Know your lines, but always bring your sides with you into the room. Casting may ask you to pick up your lines in a specific spot. Have the sides close by, just in case.

4. **All auditions are important.**
   Actors need to know that whenever they go on auditions, they are not only auditioning for the project they are called in for, but for future projects as well.

5. **Own the room.**
   When you enter the room, enter with confidence and personality. Every actor who auditions for that role will be good. Just like you, they are all professional actors. So, how do you stand out above the other actors? By making a positive, memorable impression on the casting director and their team.

Whether you earn this part or not, you want to earn a spot on the casting director's 'shortlist" of actors for this project or others.

6. **What monologue should I use?**
First off, most of the time you are going to be auditioning from sides, but if you are given the choice of a monologue, don't freak out over finding the "perfect" one. There is no such thing as the "perfect monologue." Just pick something fairly recent and relevant that represents your age and gender. That's it! Now be prepared, be confident, and own the room.

7. **Always be prepared.**
There are hundreds of reasons why you didn't properly prepare for your audition, but don't make excuses when you walk into the room. The casting director, producer, or whoever else is in the room doesn't care – at all. Prepare, prepare, prepare. If you don't take the time to prepare properly for auditions, you might as well quit the acting business. You will never have what it takes to be a long-term success.

COACHING & TRAINING

8. **Hone your craft!**
   Take classes with reputable, known acting coaches. This will help develop your skills and if the acting coach is known throughout the industry, it can bolster your résumé.

9. **Choose a regular coach.**
   Work with many coaches, but choose a regular acting coach. This person will help you develop as an actor. They will know your shortcomings and your strengths better than anyone else.

10. **Use a coach to develop a character.**
    Always work with an acting coach on character development when auditioning for a big role. Coaches will often know the casting director and may have some insight into what they are looking for from the character. Actors who prepare for the audition are in a better position to earn the part.

11. **Learn from others.**
    Watch other actors and see what they do well. Whether they are in your acting class, on stage, in television or film, or even an acting troupe, watch your colleagues and learn. Look up well-known actors and watch their audition videos online to get a better understanding of how that audition translated to the final version of the scene.

12. **Broaden your knowledge.**
    See more films, read more books, watch more plays, study more monologues, attend more classes, etc. The more you know, the better you become.

13. **Get experience.**
    Everyone asks, "How am I supposed to get experience when casting only seems to hire experienced actors?" Remember, everyone began as an inexperienced actor. Be willing to do local theatre, student films, paid and/or unpaid shorts, basically anything you can use as a legitimate credit that you can also include in your actor's reel.

FACE THE ADVERSITY

14. **The business isn't fair.**
    All actors need to know this, but many do not understand it. Yes, there are many people with very little talent who get chosen for roles over much better and more seasoned actors all the time. Why? Maybe casting wanted someone of their height or weight or hair color, whatever. The point is this, if you want to make it in the business, you just have to suck it up and understand that the business isn't fair. At some point, you will be cast in a role... and someone else will feel that it isn't fair.

15. **There is always someone better than you (even future you).**
    No matter how famous you may become in the acting business, there's always someone out there who is better than you. Other actors may be more talented or better looking, have years more experience, or have just been blessed to be luckier than you. But there isn't anything you can do about that – let it go. Just continue to work hard, train more, and seek advice, especially from those who you consider better than you. Just keep pushing forward, and never give up. Every day you get better and your efforts will eventually pay off.

16. **Get out of your own way.**
    Most of the time, you are your own worst enemy. Maybe you are lazy and procrastinate, which leads to your failure to properly prepare for an audition. Maybe you have a voice in your head that continues to tell you you're not good enough. Maybe you constantly compare yourself to actors who are nothing like you or the characters you play. Whatever the reasons, you become your own worst enemy. Take a breath, re-evaluate your path, study your craft, and, for Heaven's sake – get out of your own way!

17. **You'll never make it if you give up – so don't!**
It is easy to get frustrated in the acting business. Submitting audition after audition without earning a role can be devastating, especially to your ego. The business is hard, and many people, if not most, give up. There are tens of thousands of people, just like you – same age, same height, same race, same hair color – who are trying to break into the business right now. But as people quit trying and move on to new things, there are fewer and fewer doubles of you to choose from, so your chances of earning a role become higher and higher. So stay the course. Don't give up. You can accomplish your goals, but only if you refuse to quit.

GETTING WORK

18. **Work begets work.**
    The more you work, the more you work. So work as much as possible. It will only lead to bigger and better roles.

19. **Be versatile.**
    Don't just be the mother/father figure or the love interest; expand your abilities and show that you can become any character to make yourself more marketable and versatile.

20. **Consider working on film sets BEHIND the camera.**
    A great way to learn more about the industry is by working behind the camera. There are a ton of things actors never learn about the career path they have chosen. By working behind the camera, you get to see the inner workings of making a film. You get to see what actors look like from the director's view. You begin to understand lighting, sound, and many other technical aspects. And, if you work hard and people like you, you can increase the likelihood that you will get more opportunities to be ON camera.

21. **Network. Network. Network.**
    We've all heard the old saying, "It's not what you know, it's who you know." Well, that statement is very often true, to some extent. It tends to be true, not just in the acting business but in every business. Building a strong network of people in the business can help your career exponentially. Building relationships with other actors is great, but they are less likely to help advance your career than people who work in production jobs or in crew positions on set. Remember, other actors are your competition, and while you may be friends, they are less likely to help you get opportunities in film because they are focused on their own acting careers.

However, people in other areas of the industry love the recognition that comes with finding the "next great actor." In fact, it can have explosive effects on catapulting their career. So, search them out and network. Who you know will open doors for you. But remember, once you are inside that door, it's what you know that will get you the job.

HEADSHOTS

22. **Headshots are your #1 marketing tool.**
    Pay for quality headshots. Headshots are professionally taken. Casting can always tell the difference, so invest in yourself and your career by hiring a professional 'Actor's' headshot photographer.

23. **How often should you take headshots?**
    Adults: Take headshots as frequently as your look changes. Children: Take headshots at least annually, quite possibly every six months.

24. **Headshots should always be 8" by 10" (8×10).**
    This is the standard photo size for the industry. Never use a headshot that's larger or smaller in size, and always shoot your headshots vertically, not horizontally. Also, be sure to have high-resolution professional digital photos so you can make headshot prints if requested. The old days of having printed headshots have gotten more rare do to the popularity of online casting calls and self-taping auditions for submissions.

25. **Should headshots be color or black & white?**
    There are very, rare occasions when an actor should use anything other than color for their headshots. Black & white is often used in modeling, but not acting. Stick with color, unless instructed otherwise.

26. **Headshots should highlight your face, not your body.**
    Headshots are called headshots because they highlight your head, specifically your face. Casting directors want to see the "money maker." In most film/television scenes, the camera is focused on your face, not the rest of your body. Full-body photos are for models. Stay focused on your

face. Additionally, don't leave a large amount of space above your head in the photo. It's okay to cut off a small portion of the top of your head, as long as your face remains the focal point of the photo. However, casting may request full-body digital pictures to confirm your body type and that your physical stats match your résumé. If "digitals" are requested for an acting role, then casting will specify how to take them for their specific project. Otherwise, focus on your unique facial features, and highlight your eyes, acting has so much to do with your eyes (but that is a lesson for another time).

27. **What outfits should I wear for my headshot?**
It all depends on the character styles you are trying to portray in your headshots. Most people will have one professional/dressy photo and at least one casual photo. Dressy does not necessarily mean suit and tie, but you will likely want to wear business attire if you are trying to show that you can play a business person, politician, lawyer, etc. If you are portraying a funny/quirky character; bright shirts, glasses and crazy hair may be appropriate. Again, this is 100% your decision based on the roles you hope to gain from your headshots.

28. **MEN: Should I take pictures with or without a beard?**
The simple answer is BOTH. But again, this is solely based on character choice. However, casting agents often like to see different looks, so they know how you look depending on the image they have for the character they are casting. Some men like to do a full beard, scruffy/shadow and clean-shaven. All are good options. But keep in mind, if you take all three styles on the same day, after you have fully shaven, your face may be red. This will be obviously in your headshots, meaning you may have to shoot the latter on a different day. This is only determined by how your face reacts to shaving. If you know your face does not show

redness, by all means, take them all in one day. If it does show redness, you may want to consider coming back on a different day.

29. **Avoid tanning for at least two days before taking your headshots.**
Even if you don't easily burn, sunbathing and/or tanning beds will give your skin a redness that is obvious on camera. Even if you don't see it, the camera does, especially if you have a lighter skin tone. Simply avoid the sun for a couple of days before your photo shoot, which will allow your skin to heal before you step in front of the camera.

30. **Use strong, bold-colored backgrounds.**
In today's digital age, casting directors are most-likely finding you from a list of thumbnail photos on a computer screen. You want your headshot to jump off the screen! Using a background with color and/or texture that contrasts your face and draws the viewer's attention to your image will help you get noticed more frequently.

31. **What background colors should be avoided?**
Black backgrounds are predominantly used for theatre headshots, so try to avoid black if you are focused on film and television. Otherwise, there are not any colors that should be avoided, as long as they are used in the proper context for the look you are trying to portray. For instance, children and teens will often use vibrant colors like light blues, yellows, or even pinks. However, adults should avoid these, unless their headshot is intended to portray a goofy or quirky character. If you are trying to portray a sinister or rugged character, a darker color may be okay, unless you have a darker skin tone. The same is true for people with a lighter or pale skin tone. They should avoid lighter colors like white or yellow. Remember, you always want

something that will allow your face to be the focal point. Don't allow your face to blend in with your background color and disappear.

RÉSUMÉ

38. **How do I make my résumé stand out?**
    Just like headshots, you want your résumé to grab a casting director's attention. Don't use the standard black-and-white format everyone else does; add a hint of color. We're not suggesting you use colored paper or add a background color. That's way too over the top. But having colored lines that separate sections, colored text for your name and personal information at the top, a sidebar that includes your special talents or skills, or even a small full-color image of your headshot in the top left or right of the page can help your résumé carry the pizzazz needed to become memorable and make its way into the audition stack. In truth, there is no industry standard. However, there are specific layouts that are more accepted and effective in different markets (commercial, film, television, theater, etc). It is very common for actors to have several different formats for different target jobs they wish to book.

39. **What to include in your résumé.**
    - Full Name (or stage name)
    - Representation (if you have an agent and/or manager)
    - Contact information (phone and email)
    - Physical Attributes (height, weight, hair and eye color)
    - Film Credits
    - Television Credits
    - Commercial Credits (list only if you are still building your résumés and have limited film and television credits)
    - Theatre Credit (only if you are looking for theatre roles)
    - Education and Training
    - Special Skills

40. **Proper order of film credit categories.**
    Lead / Supporting Lead / Supporting / Featured

Background and Extra roles should not be listed on your résumé – ever.

41. **Proper order of television credit categories.**
Series Regular / Recurring / Guest Star / Co-Star / Cameo
Again, never list Background and Extra roles on your résumé.

SELF-TAPING

42. **Recording a proper self-tape audition.**
    Hold your camera horizontally (left to right, not up and down) and frame yourself from just above the navel to just above the head. Also, your filming background should be neutral in color (gray or blue are preferred) and well-lit so that you minimize shadowing. Finally, wear a form-fitting shirt, but avoid patterns and colors that will match the background behind you and wash you out.

43. **Purchase a quality camera.**
    A good camera will allow you to get quality footage from your self-taping sessions. Look for a camera that has an external microphone connection.

44. **Can you use my cell phone camera?**
    The simple answer is yes. Most cell phones are equipped with a sufficient camera for self-taping. When you are just starting out and on a tight budget, use what you have. However, you must make sure to follow all the same filming requirements and utilize quality sound and lighting.

45. **Purchase a quality external microphone.**
    Your sound is just as important as your video. Bad audio will kill any audition, even one with great acting. Make sure your camera has a good microphone, but if it has an external microphone jack, even better. Purchase a quality external microphone and use it.

46. **Purchase quality lights and a proper backdrop.**
    You can get an entire professional photography set for a very, affordable price. Simply do a web search for "professional lighting set" and you will find options with complete backdrop frames, multiple backdrop colors and

multiple, filtered lights (usually 3-5) and light stands. If you don't have lighting equipment or can't afford it yet, make sure to have ample amounts of natural lighting – absolutely NO fluorescent lighting. Proper lighting will make your audition look like it was recorded in a professional studio, so take the time to make sure you get it right.

TECHNOLOGY

47. **Get a personal website.**
    It's a great idea for actors to have personal websites. There are many websites that allow you to build a site, even if you have no design experience.

48. **Join IMDb Pro.**
    If not before, consider joining IMDb Pro as soon as you have a credit. Many professionals within the industry will look up your credentials on IMDb.

49. **Join audition websites.**
    Utilize websites like Actors Access, Casting Networks, Casting Frontier, Backstage, etc. These sites will give you access to professional auditions in television, film, commercials, and theatre.

50. **Join social media groups for people in the film/television industry.**
    Social media sites have many groups, both public and private that solely focus on the entertainment industry. Join as many as you can and follow them closely. Some groups are for actors, some are for directors, producers, writers, cinematographers, and crew, and many are for all of the above. If you watch closely enough, members will provide tips and industry insights. Additionally, some may post information about upcoming auditions for their own projects.

51. **Build your followers on social media sites.**
    In today's technology age, many actors get their first big roles because they have a large social media following. This may seem frivolous, but actors with a large number of followers have a built-in fan base that is likely to follow

their projects or buy their merchandise. This is why they call these people "influencers." Having well-managed social media sites with many followers is a huge benefit to your career pursuits.

WRAP-UP

I hope you found these tips to be helpful and they provided you some industry insights you didn't otherwise know. This additional knowledge will provide you a head start on many of your fellow actors, giving you better chances and more opportunities to succeed in this crazy business we call acting.

Remember, never give up. Stay the course. Persistence and improvement is the key to long-term success in any industry, especially acting. Don't allow yourself to become discouraged by failure. This is an industry of numbers. For every "no" you receive, you are one step closer to a "yes."

Every actor forges their own pathway as they pursue their career. Many begin as a child performing for family members in costumes or make-up. Others may make their way through the theatre performing plays or musicals, or inspired classics from Shakespeare or Wilde. Some discover or revisit their passion later in life after their children are grown and/or they have retired from their careers.

However, no matter what path you take toward your career as an actor, rest assured you will face obstacles. Many will seem insurmountable, but they aren't. You can and will find a way to clear the obstacles and knock down the walls that stand in your way. Simply believe in yourself and continue to learn along your journey.

Knowledge is power. I can't stress that enough. Working, training, and studying your selected career field will lead to success at whatever level you desire. As a bonus, I have included **101 Terms Every Actor Should Know**. Whether you are new to the business or a veteran, understanding the terminology used in the business and while on set, gives you an upper hand on the competition. It makes you a better actor and leads to you being referred to as a revered term in this industry – a professional.

101 TERMS EVERY ACTOR SHOULD KNOW

1st A.D.: The right-hand person to the director. Assists the director by coordinating all production activity and supervising the cast and crew.

2nd A.D.: The right-hand person to the 1st A.D. They prepare the daily call sheet and supervise actors and crew. Is responsible for actors being where they need to be.

BONUS SECTION

AEA: AEA or Actors' Equity Association is the labor union that represents American theatre actors and stage managers.

AGVA: AVGA or the American Guild of Variety Artists is an AFL-CIO affiliated labor union that represents performing artists and stage managers for live performances in the variety field. This includes singers & dancers in touring shows, theme park performers, skaters, circus performers, comedians & stand-up comics, as well as cabaret and club artists.

AGMA: AGMA, or the American Guild of Musical Artists, is the American labor union that represents opera singers, ballet dancers, opera directors, opera and dance company production personnel, and figure skaters.

Action: What the director says to indicate the camera is rolling and a scene has started.

Ad-Lib: When an actor goes off-script and is expected to improvise in a scene.

Adjustment: A change in direction regarding the playing of certain material.

Advance: An amount of money paid before work has started to secure a professional's place on a production.

Aside: A bit of dialogue directed only at the audience on stage, unheard by other characters.

Audition: The tryout for a role in a film, television show or stage production.

Back to One: A verbal cue indicating actors should return to where they started a scene.

Background/Extra Performers: Extras in a production, frequently used in the background of a scene.

Background Casting Director: The person responsible for booking all of the background/extra performers, stand-ins and photo-doubles.

Backstage: The area behind the stage in a production or unseen by the audience.

Bit Part: A role in which there is direct interaction with the principal actors, but no more than five lines of dialogue.

Beat: A deliberate pause in dialogue or action.

Black Out: When all stage lights are shut down.

Blocking: The physical movements of actors, and sometimes crew, orchestrated in a scene.

Booking: A firm commitment to the performer to do a specific job.

Breaking Character: When an actor stops acting and steps out of their role.

Budget: The amount of money available for the making of a production.

Call Back: A second audition, in which an actor is 'called back' to show their skills again.

Call Sheet: The list of schedules for all cast and crew in a production.

Call Time: The time that an actor must be on set.

Camera Left: When performers take up the left side of the shot from the camera operator's perspective.

Camera Right: When performers take up the right side of the shot from the camera operator's perspective.

Camera ready: The state of and actor being ready for filming, with hair, makeup and costuming done.

Casting: The process of choosing the performers for a production, done by the casting director, director or other industry professionals.

Casting Director: The person responsible for auditioning and choosing principal performers for consideration by the producers and/or director of a production.

Closing Off: When an actor turns away from the audience.

Cold Reading: In an audition, when an actor is asked to use material they haven't studied or seen previously.

Commission: A portion of an actor's earnings taken by an agent or manager.

Craft services: The on-set table containing food for cast and crew on a production.

Cue: A signal for an actor to begin or continue their performing.

Cut: The verbal cue for filming to stop.

Dailies: Raw footage shot on the same day.

Day Player: A principal performer hired on a daily basis, rather than a long term contract.

Demo Reel: A compilation of highlights of an actor's previous on-camera roles.

DIT: This is the digital imaging technician who has a number of important technical roles on set, but their primary responsibility is to transfer footage from the camera (and often audio) department's memory cards to multiple backup drives, in order to avoid loss of recorded footage.

Dialect: A distinct regional or linguistic speech pattern.

Director: The person who coordinates all of the artistic and technical aspects of a production.

Director of Photography (D.P.): Supervises all decisions regarding lighting, lenses, filters, color, camera set-ups, the camera crew and the processing of the film.

Distribution: The process of making a movie available to an audience through theatrical release, television broadcast, streaming platforms, DVD/Blu-ray sales and other digital formats.

Downstage: The section of the stage that is closest to the audience.

Dress Rehearsal or Run-Through: A rehearsal in full costume, usually right before a first performance.

Feature: A full-length film.

Fourth Wall: The imaginary area that separates an actor from the audience/viewers. The fourth wall is broken when an actor makes an aside directly to the audience or camera.

Holding: The designated area where background/extra performers report and stay while waiting to go on set.

Hot set: A set that is ready for filming.

Improvisation: When an actor performs spontaneously with no script.

Lead Actor/Actress: The main protagonist in the production. It is typically the largest role.

Mark: The exact position assigned to an actor on set.

Monologue: The term for a lengthy speech given by a single actor in a scene.

Motivation: The 'why' behind a character's actions.

Off Book: When an actor has their lines completely memorized and does not need to refer to a script.

On Book: When an actor has not yet memorized their script.

On Hold: When a casting director identifies that they want an actor for a production, but has not yet formally hired them.

Open Call: A day for auditions open to anyone.

Opening Up: When an actor turns toward the audience or camera.

Out of Frame: When a performer is outside of the camera's field of view.

Pace: The speed at which a scene unfolds, or the speed at which actors deliver their lines.

Photo Double: An actor who resembles a principal actor who is used to perform on camera in place of that person.

Pick Up: When a scene is started at a place aside from its beginning.

Places: A command to inform performers to take their assigned positions on stage.

Points: Someone is moving a piece of equipment (such as light stands) that has pointed ends or extensions. This a warning to make room and/or watch out for your own safety.

Principal Actor: A performer with lines.

Production Assistant (P.A.): Assists with all aspects of production. Depending on need, some work in the production office, while others work on set.

Props: The objects used by actors in a scene.

Quiet on Set: Everyone on set should be as quiet as possible. In most cases, this means cameras and audio are about to start rolling.

Room Tone: All members of a production need to be completely silent while audio captures sound from the location of filming. This room tone may need in the case of ADR or other voiceovers to keep consistent background audio within a film.

Rush call: Last-minute booking of actors or extras.

SAG-AFTRA: SAG-AFTRA or the Screen Actors Guild - American Federation of Television and Radio Artists is the labor union that represents film and television actors, broadcast journalists, radio personalities, recording artists, singers, voice actors and other media professionals.

Sides: Pages from a script used to audition or shoot with.

Script: The written form of a film or production, containing all actors' lines and directions.

Slate: A quick statement of a performer's information before an audition begins.

Soliloquy: A long speech by an actor without anyone else on stage, sometimes directed at the audience.

Spiking the Lens: When an actor looks directly into the camera during filming.

Stage Left: The area to the actor's left.

Stage right: The area to the actor's right.

Stage Manager: This person handles the organization of a theatrical production, which includes being the link between director and crew and the actors and production management.

Stand-in: A background/extra performer who is used as a substitute for the principal actor for the purpose of setting up an upcoming shot. This allows the director of photography to set the lights and rehearse the movement that will take place in front of the camera.

Standby: The verbal indication that actors should be ready and awaiting their cue.

Standard Union Contract: The contract approved by the unions and offered to performers prior to the job.

Striking: This is a warning that someone is preparing to turn on a light. Avert your face to avoid direct eye contact.

Stunt Person: A specially trained performer who performs stunts on camera.

Supporting Actor/Actress: A speaking role that is less than that of a lead actor, but larger than a bit part.

Take: A shot in progress.

VFX: Visual effects.

Upstage: The part of the stage farthest away from the audience.

Understudy: A performer hired to do a role only if the featured actor is unable to perform; used primarily in theatre.

Union: This indicates work on a production only for members of the particular union concerned.

Upgrade: The promotion of a background/extra performer in a scene to the category of principal performer (the performer is given lines).

Voucher: The time slip with all of the pertinent info needed for a performer to be paid after working.

Wardrobe Department: This department handles all of the costuming for the actors performing in the production. They hold fittings for performers to dress them specifically or give instructions as to what type of clothing and colors are acceptable for the actors to wear.

Waiver: Union approved permission for a non-union performer to be allowed to work as union for the day.

Walk Away Lunch: A meal break in which cast and crew are responsible for getting their own lunch.

Wardrobe Allowance: A fee paid to on-camera talent for the use and cleaning of the performer's own clothing.

Wardrobe: An appointment in which the wardrobe department meets with the talent to prepare the clothing they will wear in the production.

Weather Permit Call: Due to weather conditions, the production company has the option to release the talent from working that day for a reduced rate of pay.

Wrap: The end of filming for a day.

www.ingramcontent.com/pod-product-compliance
Lightning Source LLC
Chambersburg PA
CBHW070048070426
42449CB00012BA/3188